The KidHaven Health Library

What Happens When Someone Has

ALLERGIES?

By Katie Kawa

Published in 2020 by
KidHaven Publishing, an Imprint of Greenhaven Publishing, LLC
353 3rd Avenue
Suite 255
New York, NY 10010

Designer: Andrea Davison-Bartolotta
Editor: Katie Kawa

Photo credits: Cover, p. 7 Dmytro Zinkevych/Shutterstock.com; p. 4 Andrey_Popov/ Shutterstock.com; p. 5 Lyubov Kobyakova/Shutterstock.com; p. 6 Likoper/Shutterstock.com; p. 8 Shidlovski/Shutterstock.com; p. 9 Sudowoodo/Shutterstock.com; p. 11 Africa Studio/ Shutterstock.com; p. 12 greenland/Shutterstock.com; p. 13 (right) BlurryMe/Shutterstock.com; p. 13 (left) konmesa/Shutterstock.com; p. 14 Rocketclips, Inc./Shutterstock.com; p. 15 Lyudmila Tetera/Shutterstock.com; p. 17 (graphic organizer) Khvost/Shutterstock.com; p. 17 (bottom left, top middle left, top middle right, bottom middle left) New Africa/Shutterstock.com; p. 17 (top left, top right, bottom middle right, bottom right) Evan Lorne/Shutterstock.com; p. 18 Peter Dazeley/ Photographer's Choice/Getty Images Plus/Getty Images; pp. 19, 29 Monkey Business Images/ Shutterstock.com; p. 21 (top) Alexander Raths/Shutterstock.com; p. 21 (bottom) Anthony Ricci/ Shutterstock.com; p. 22 Yuganov Konstantin/Shutterstock.com; p. 23 JPC-PROD/Shutterstock.com; p. 25 Katherine Frey/The Washington Post via Getty Images; p. 26 lev radin/Shutterstock.com.

Cataloging-in-Publication Data

Names: Kawa, Katie.
Title: What happens when someone has allergies? / Katie Kawa.
Description: New York : KidHaven Publishing, 2020. | Series: The KidHaven health library | Includes glossary and index.
Identifiers: ISBN 9781534532595 (pbk.) | ISBN 9781534532465 (library bound) | ISBN 9781534532625 (6 pack) | ISBN 9781534532526 (ebook)
Subjects: LCSH: Allergy–Juvenile literature.
Classification: LCC RC584.K39 2020 | DDC 616.97–dc23

Printed in the United States of America

Some of the images in this book illustrate individuals who are models. The depictions do not imply actual situations or events.

CPSIA compliance information: Batch #BW20KL: For further information contact Greenhaven Publishing LLC, New York, New York at 1-844-317-7404.

Please visit our website, www.greenhavenpublishing.com. For a free color catalog of all our high-quality books, call toll free 1-844-317-7404 or fax 1-844-317-7405.

Contents

ALLERGIES AREN'T FUN!

Spending time outside is fun for many people. For others, however, it can cause sneezing, **itchy** skin, and even trouble breathing. These people have allergies—health problems that happen when their body treats something harmless, such as grass, as a danger that needs to be attacked.

Outdoor allergies are common, but so are allergies to things such as pets, foods, and medicines. Allergies can make people uncomfortable and can make dealing with everyday life hard. In some cases, allergies can make people very sick and send them to the hospital.

Taking Allergies Seriously

An allergy is a chronic health problem. This means it's a problem that doesn't go away or that happens often. Many people live with allergies for a long time. In some cases, they don't get the help they need because they don't think having an allergy is a serious health problem. However, allergies should be taken seriously, and that often means getting treatment from a doctor. People with allergies also need support from their family members and friends—just like people with any other health problem.

Although allergies can be unpleasant and even scary to deal with, they can often be treated. With the right treatment, or care, people with allergies can play outside or hug their pets without any problems.

More than 50 million Americans deal with allergies every year. Allergies affect adults and kids. In fact, more than 6 million kids in the United States have at least one allergy.

INSIDE THE IMMUNE SYSTEM

An allergic reaction is what happens to someone's body when they have an allergy. It starts when a person comes in contact with an allergen, which is a thing they're allergic to. They might do this by breathing in pollen, eating a peanut, or being stung by a bee. Next, their immune system, which protects the body from germs, goes into action. This happens because their body mistakenly thinks the allergen is a harmful germ.

Running in Families

Allergies sometimes run in families. This has led scientists to believe there are genes that make someone more likely to have certain allergies. Genes are the building blocks of living things that control **traits** such as eye color and how likely someone is to have certain health problems. It's helpful to know your family medical history, including any allergies that run in your family. This can make it easier for doctors to know how likely you are to have an allergy.

The immune system makes antibodies, which get rid of germs. When a person has an allergy, their immune system produces an antibody called Immunoglobulin E (IgE). Different types of IgE antibodies **react** to different types of allergens. This is why some people are allergic to only one thing, while others are allergic to many things.

If someone is allergic to cats, their body produces IgE when it comes in contact with a cat. The immune system remembers what it thinks is harmful, so every time that person pets a cat, their body will produce IgE, causing an allergic reaction.

IgE's job is to activate cells called mast cells. They store and make chemicals that help the body get rid of what it thinks is a harmful invader—something that's not supposed to be there. One of the chemicals in mast cells is histamine. When histamine is released, or sent out, it increases the amount of blood sent to an area the immune system thinks needs help. This is known as inflammation. In the case of someone with an allergy, inflammation is generally what causes an allergic reaction.

Inflammation can cause parts of the body to swell or turn red. People with allergies want to stop inflammation before it starts. This is why they often take medicines called antihistamines, which stop histamine from being released.

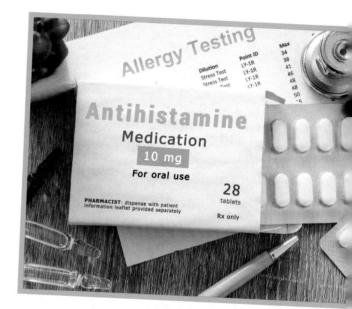

Can Allergies Change with Age?

Some allergies can last for a person's entire life. However, allergies often change as a person gets older. Kids sometimes outgrow their allergies. For example, up to 80 percent of kids outgrow their allergy to milk or eggs by the time they're in their late teens. In other cases, though, adults can start to have new allergies as they get older. Scientists are still working to better understand why some allergies seem to change with age.

Common Allergic Reactions

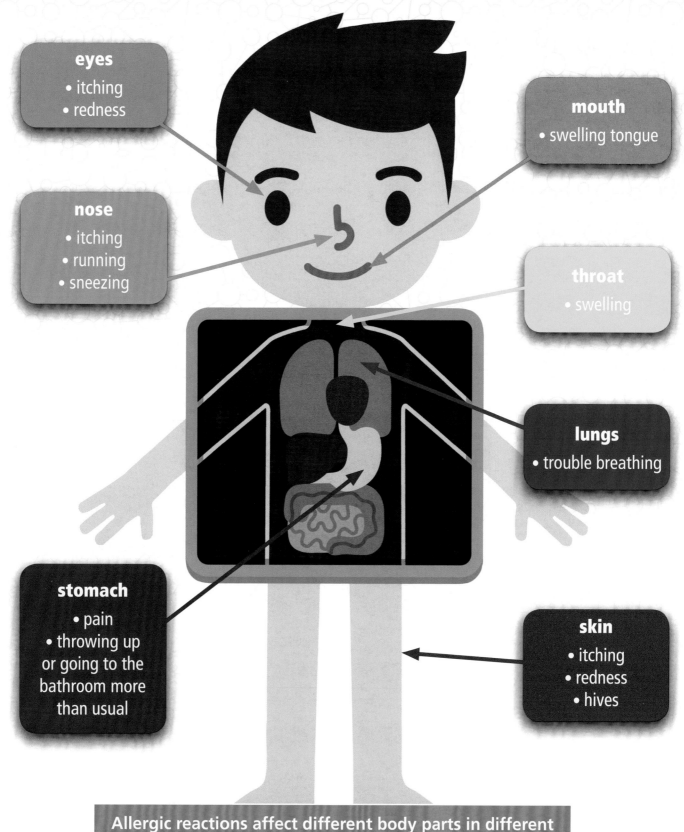

eyes
- itching
- redness

mouth
- swelling tongue

nose
- itching
- running
- sneezing

throat
- swelling

lungs
- trouble breathing

stomach
- pain
- throwing up or going to the bathroom more than usual

skin
- itching
- redness
- hives

Allergic reactions affect different body parts in different ways. These are some common signs of an allergic reaction. A person might only show one of these signs, but that can be enough to cause serious health problems.

THE NOSE KNOWS

Many people who have allergies often say they have hay fever. That's another name for allergic rhinitis, or a nasal allergy. It's caused by inflammation in the nose that happens after someone breathes in an allergen such as **mold** or pollen.

Symptoms, or signs, of nasal allergies include sneezing and an itchy nose. In some cases, the body produces more mucus to try to get rid of the allergen. Mucus is a **fluid** that helps keep harmful things out of the lungs. When the body produces too

Causes of Allergic Rhinitis

tree pollen

grass pollen

weed pollen

These are the most common causes of allergic rhinitis. Allergies to pollen are often known as outdoor allergies. Allergies to pets, mold, feathers, and dust mites are often considered indoor allergies.

pet dander or bodily fluids

mold

feathers, such as those used in pillows

dust mites—small creatures that live in dust

much mucus or if the mucus becomes too thick, it can cause a runny nose, a stuffy nose, or an uncomfortable feeling of it going down the throat. These symptoms can last all year or only during certain seasons, which is a condition known as seasonal allergies.

When Pets Cause Problems

Some people are allergic to certain pets, such as dogs or cats. Although people often think they're allergic to the animal's fur or hair, the actual allergen is often the animal's bodily fluids or dander—dead skin cells. Pet allergies often affect the nose and eyes, but they can also affect the lungs and cause breathing problems. In some cases, people who have a pet allergy have to find their pet a new home so they can feel better.

SKIN ALLERGIES

Another body part that's commonly affected by allergies is the skin. When someone has an allergy, they sometimes break out in hives, which are small bumps on the skin that can be very itchy. Hives—especially hives all over the body—can sometimes be a sign of a serious allergic reaction.

The Eyes Have It

Allergies can affect a person's eyes too. If an allergen gets into a person's eyes, the inflammation that happens can cause their eyes to become red and itchy. Sometimes, their eyes might also get watery, or they might have a burning feeling like when soap gets in your eyes. Swollen eyelids can also be a sign of an allergic reaction affecting the eyes. Special eye drops are often used to treat these symptoms.

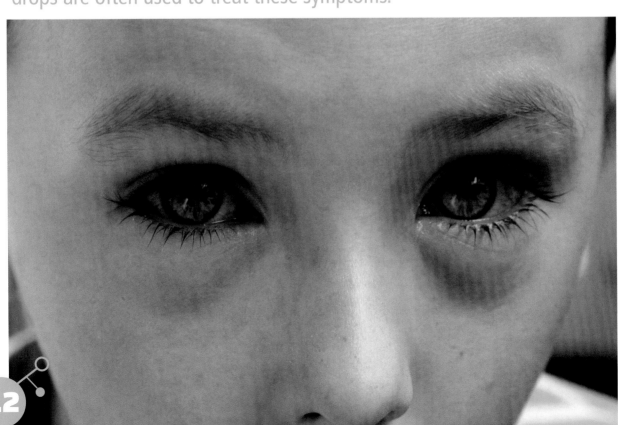

Eczema is another skin condition that's often caused by allergies. It doesn't always look the same. Some people with eczema have areas of flaky, dry skin, while others have red rashes that are very itchy. Eczema often affects kids with allergies, but adults can have it too.

People are sometimes allergic to things that touch their skin, such as rubber gloves and bandages. These products are made with latex. A latex allergy can cause hives, swollen eyes, and breathing problems.

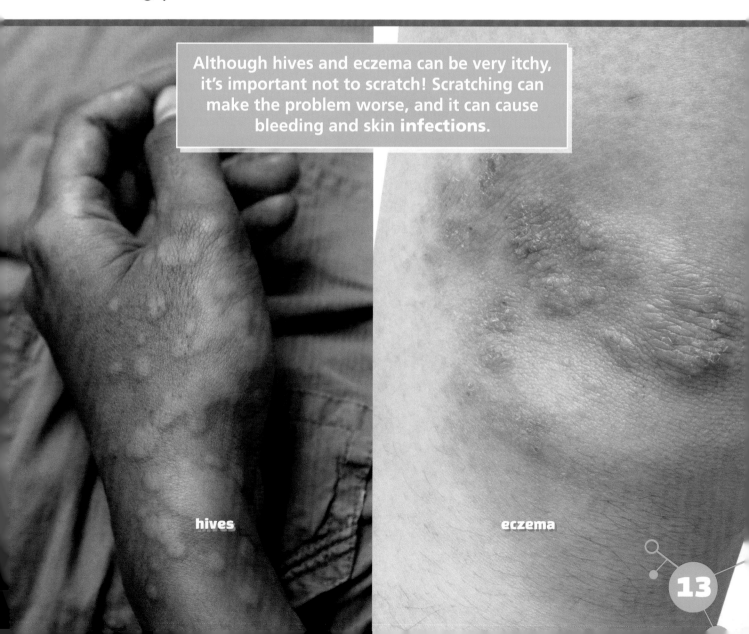

Although hives and eczema can be very itchy, it's important not to scratch! Scratching can make the problem worse, and it can cause bleeding and skin **infections**.

hives

eczema

BITES AND STINGS

Some people are afraid of bugs because they think bugs look scary. Other people are afraid of bugs because they're allergic to them. They might be allergic to stinging bugs, such as bees or wasps, or biting bugs, such as mosquitoes or fleas. In some cases, people are allergic to bugs that don't sting or bite. Dust mites are one example; cockroaches are another.

Drug Allergies

A drug allergy happens when a person's immune system thinks that medicine that's supposed to help them feel better is actually harmful. Because medicine often affects the whole body, so does an allergic reaction to medicine. It can cause itching and hives all over the body, swelling, and shortness of breath. If you have a drug allergy, it's important to tell your family and your doctors so they know what medicines you can and can't take.

An allergic reaction to a bug bite or sting causes more than just the usual pain, itching, and swelling that most people experience. It can cause hives all over the body and breathing problems.

If a person has an allergy to a bug, it's important to take it seriously. They need to stay away from that kind of bug to stay safe and healthy!

Many people are afraid of bees and wasps because they don't want to be stung. That fear is even greater for people who are allergic to these bugs.

THE FACTS ABOUT FOOD ALLERGIES

Many kinds of allergies have been on the rise in recent years. These include food allergies, which affect kids more often than adults.

Common food allergy symptoms include hives, an itchy mouth, trouble breathing, and swelling in the lips, face, or tongue. Stomach problems, including pain and feeling sick to your stomach, can also happen. If you have any of these problems after eating something, tell an adult right away. Some food allergies are mild, but others can be very serious.

Some restaurants offer special menus for people with food allergies so they know they can eat safely. In addition, packages of food often list possible allergens. If you have a food allergy, it's important to be as informed, or educated, as possible about what you can and can't eat.

Celiac Disease

Some people can't eat certain foods for reasons other than allergies. For example, celiac disease is a serious disease, or sickness, in which the immune system attacks the **small intestine** when people eat gluten. Because gluten is found in wheat, people with celiac disease get sick when they eat bread and other foods made with wheat. They have to stay away from these foods or they get stomach pain and other harmful symptoms.

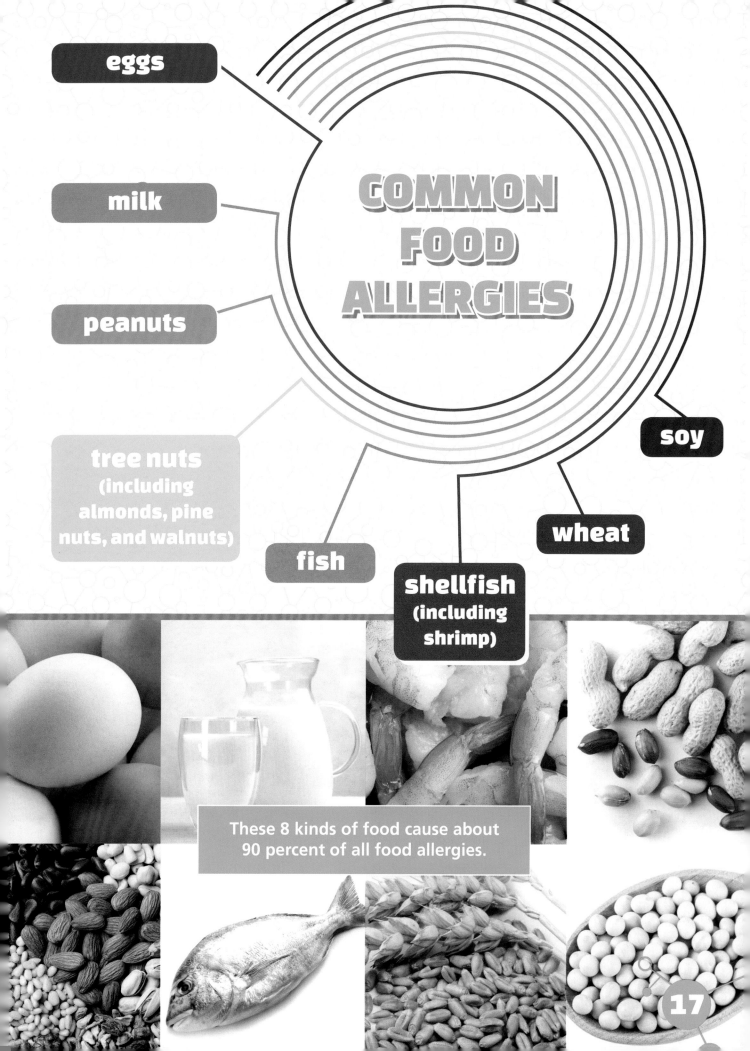

COMMON FOOD ALLERGIES

eggs

milk

peanuts

tree nuts (including almonds, pine nuts, and walnuts)

fish

shellfish (including shrimp)

soy

wheat

These 8 kinds of food cause about 90 percent of all food allergies.

A DANGEROUS REACTION

Most people with allergies have reactions that make them uncomfortable and often unhappy, but they don't cause serious health problems. However, one kind of allergic reaction can put someone's life in danger if it's not treated quickly. This kind of reaction is known as anaphylaxis.

The Importance of an EpiPen

Someone who's been treated for anaphylaxis is often given a device called an EpiPen to help them if it happens again. An EpiPen injects, or puts, epinephrine directly into their body. Epinephrine is a chemical that reverses the effects of anaphylaxis by raising the body's heart rate and blood pressure and making it easier to breathe. A person is supposed to carry their EpiPen at all times. It's also helpful for their close friends, family members, and teachers to know how to use it.

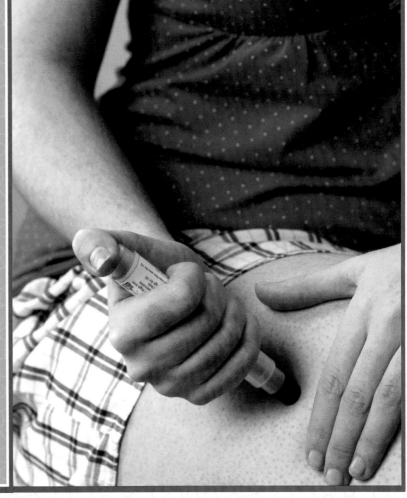

Hives and swelling all over the body are common symptoms of anaphylaxis. In addition, people experiencing anaphylaxis often have trouble breathing and swallowing. In some cases, their blood pressure and heart rate drop to dangerous levels, which can cause them to faint.

It's important for someone having this kind of allergic reaction to get medical help as soon as possible. If you or someone you're with is experiencing any of these symptoms, tell a trusted adult or call 911 right away.

After someone experiences a serious allergic reaction such as anaphylaxis, their doctor often comes up with an **emergency** treatment plan in case it happens again. This plan should be shared with teachers, coaches, and anyone else who might need to put it into action.

TESTING FOR ALLERGIES

When someone thinks they have allergies, they often go to a doctor called an allergist. An allergist uses special tests to find out what someone is allergic to.

Some people get a blood test, which tests for certain antibodies in the blood. The most common kind of allergy test, however, is a skin test. In one kind of skin test, a doctor puts certain allergens on the skin and scratches the skin to get the allergens into the body. In another kind of test, a doctor injects allergens under the skin. For a patch test, a patch with different allergens is placed on the skin. If the skin reacts with swelling or redness to certain allergens during any of these tests, the allergist will know that's what their patient is allergic to.

Keeping an Allergy Diary

Allergists often ask their patients about their lives to find out what kinds of allergens they might come in contact with. They also ask about allergy symptoms. A good way to give them all the facts they need is to write down what symptoms you experience and what you were doing when you experienced them. This is especially helpful for finding food allergies. You can keep track of this by writing in a diary or using a smartphone app.

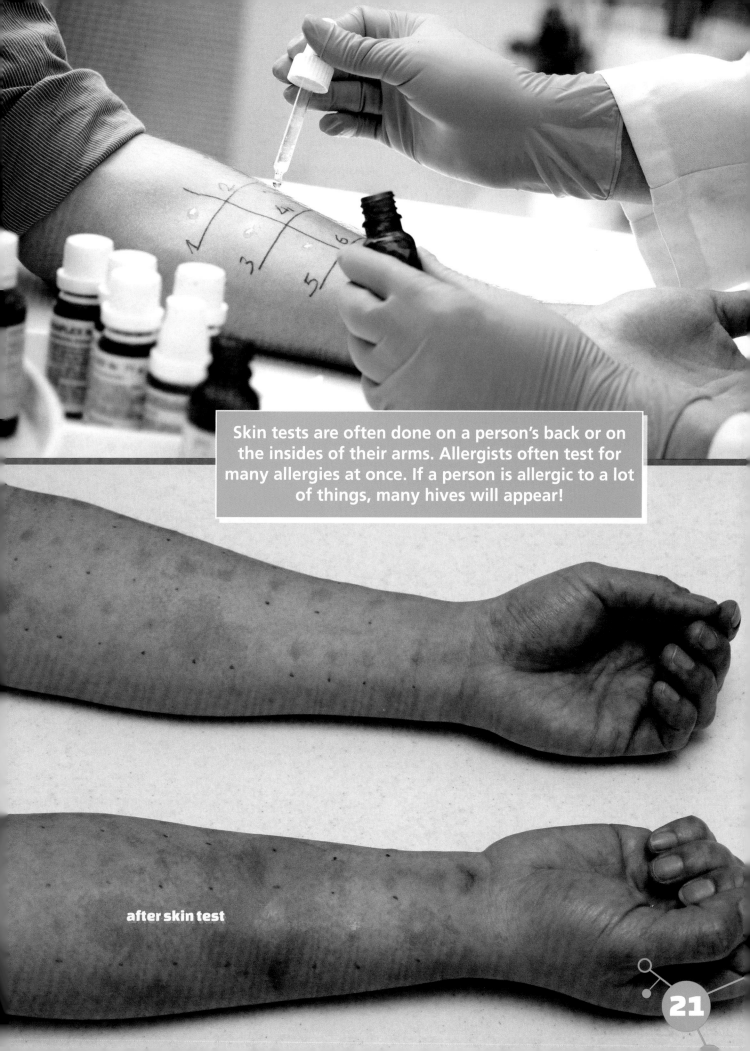

Skin tests are often done on a person's back or on the insides of their arms. Allergists often test for many allergies at once. If a person is allergic to a lot of things, many hives will appear!

after skin test

FEELING BETTER

If a person's allergy test shows they have allergies, the next step is deciding how to treat them. The best way to stop allergy symptoms is to avoid the allergens causing them. That sometimes means getting rid of a pet, keeping certain plants out of the house, or staying away from certain foods.

A Clean House Can Help!

Someone who has an allergy to mold, dust mites, or other indoor allergens can help themselves feel better by making small changes around the house. Keeping the house clean and as dust-free as possible is a good place to start. Carpets also trap a lot of dust mites. If they can't be taken out, then using a special **vacuum cleaner** can keep people from breathing in dust mites. Mold can be reduced by using a fan in the bathroom to keep it dry.

In many cases, though, it's hard to avoid allergens such as pollen because a person can't stay inside forever. People who can't avoid their allergens often take medicine to stop their allergy symptoms. These medicines include antihistamines, nasal sprays, and creams for skin allergies.

Some of these medicines can be bought over the counter, which means a doctor doesn't have to **prescribe** them. However, someone with allergies should always talk to their doctor before starting a new allergy medicine.

Many allergy medicines are safe for kids to use too.

ALLERGY SHOTS

Some people can't avoid their allergens, and they don't get enough help from medicine. When this happens, they often try allergy shots next. Allergy shots are a kind of treatment called immunotherapy, which changes how the immune system reacts to allergens.

A tiny amount of an allergen is injected under a patient's skin. This allows the immune system to get used to the allergen being in the body, so it won't react to it anymore. In order for the immune system to get used to the allergen, larger amounts of it need to be injected each time a patient gets their shots. This is called the build-up phase, and it lasts for a few months. After that, smaller amounts of the allergen can be used with more time between the shots.

Under the Tongue

Some kinds of allergies, such as allergies to certain kinds of pollen and dust mites, can be treated with a kind of immunotherapy that doesn't **involve** shots. Instead, patients are given a **tablet** with a small amount of an allergen in it. Then, they place the tablet under their tongue. This allows the allergen to get into their body so their immune system can get used to it. This kind of immunotherapy can only treat one allergy at a time.

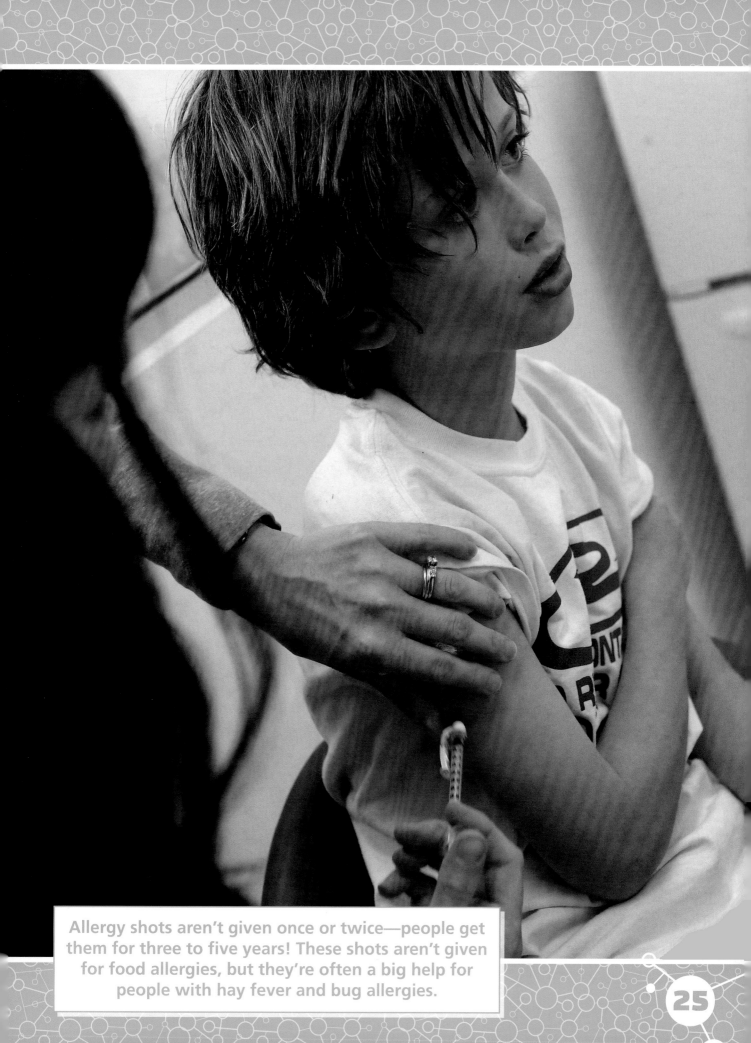

Allergy shots aren't given once or twice—people get them for three to five years! These shots aren't given for food allergies, but they're often a big help for people with hay fever and bug allergies.

YOU CAN HELP!

As the number of kids with allergies continues to rise, schools are working hard to help them. This is especially true for kids with food allergies, such as peanut allergies. Teachers and other school officials often work with parents to come up with a plan that helps kids with allergies feel safe and included in school activities, such as lunchtime and birthday celebrations. Some schools are even nut-free!

If you know someone with an allergy, you can do your part to help them avoid allergens. For example, you can play inside with them if they have pollen allergies, or you can make sure any snacks you share with them won't cause an allergic reaction.

Ariana's Allergies

Even famous people can have allergies! For example, in 2019, singer Ariana Grande found out she was allergic to tomatoes. She had a bad allergic reaction that caused her throat to feel like it was closing. It was so serious that she had to cancel part of her tour because of problems with her throat. Doctors used this story to remind people that adults can get food allergies too, even if they weren't allergic to certain foods as a kid.

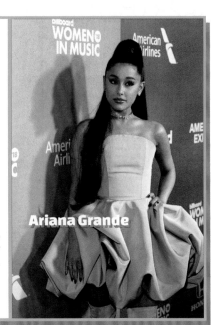

Ariana Grande

It's good to learn about your friends' and family members' allergies. Knowing what to do during an allergic reaction can save someone's life!

How can you help someone with allergies?

! Learn about what causes their allergies, and help them avoid those things.

! If they have a food allergy, ask what kinds of foods they can and can't eat, and follow what they tell you exactly.

! Ask them if you should know their emergency treatment plan, and help them practice putting that plan into action.

! If they're having an allergic reaction, tell a trusted adult right away. If the reaction is serious and you can't find an adult, call 911.

! Treat them with respect, and remind them that having allergies doesn't have to stop them from having fun!

These are just some of the ways you can help someone who lives with allergies. Having allergies can be hard, but support from family members and friends makes it a lot easier.

KNOW YOUR BODY

If you have allergies, it might not seem fair to have to stay away from certain foods or pets. However, it's what many people need to do to avoid a serious allergic reaction. In some cases, people grow out of their allergies, so there's hope that they won't last forever.

If you think you have allergies but haven't seen a doctor about them, talk to a parent or guardian about visiting an allergist. You might be able to get the treatment you need to feel better.

Knowing as much as you can about your own body, including any allergies you might have, is an important part of taking care of yourself. It can help you stay safe, healthy, and happy now and in the future.

Understanding Why

Scientists are working hard to better understand why the number of people with allergies has gone up so much in recent years. One idea they have is that we're too clean now! Some scientists believe that kids need to be exposed to more germs so their immune systems can learn the difference between what's harmful and what's not. However, other scientists believe rising allergy rates are caused by the use of certain medicines or a combination of things.

People with allergies can still have fun! With the right treatment, they may even be able to enjoy things, such as playing outside, that used to cause an allergic reaction.

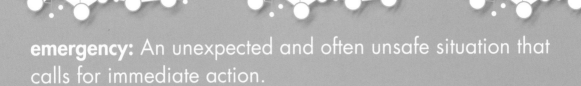

Glossary

emergency: An unexpected and often unsafe situation that calls for immediate action.

fluid: A substance that flows freely like water.

infection: A sickness caused by germs entering the body.

involve: To have or include as a part of something.

itchy: Having an unpleasant feeling that makes someone want to scratch.

mold: A fuzzy growth of fungus that often forms on damp material.

prescribe: To officially tell someone to use a medical treatment.

react: To do something because of something else that happens.

small intestine: The long, narrow, upper part of the intestine that breaks down food so it can be used by the body.

tablet: Something small and round that contains medicine that a person puts into their body.

trait: A quality that makes one person or thing different from another.

vacuum cleaner: An electrical device that cleans things by sucking up dirt and dust.

WEBSITES

KidsHealth: Learning About Allergies

kidshealth.org/en/kids/allergies.html

The KidsHealth website explains allergies in a way that's easy to understand and has links to other pages about food allergies, hives, and the immune system.

Kids with Food Allergies: Recipes and Diet

www.kidswithfoodallergies.org/page/recipes-diet.aspx

This website offers many fun and tasty recipes that are free of common food allergens.

BOOKS

Duhig, Holly. *Understanding Allergies.* New York, NY: PowerKids Press, 2019.

Gulati, Annette. *Life with Food Allergies.* Mankato, MN: Child's World, 2019.

Jorgensen, Katrina. *No Peanuts, No Problem!: Easy and Delicious Nut-Free Recipes for Kids with Allergies.* North Mankato, MN: Capstone Press, 2017.

Index